AnimalWays

Bears

AnimalWays

Bears

REBECCA STEFOFF

BENCHMARK **B**OOKS

MARSHALL CAVENDISH
NEW YORK

With thanks to Dr. Dan Wharton,
director of the Central Park Wildlife Center,
for his expert reading of this manuscript.

Benchmark Books
Marshall Cavendish Corporation
99 White Plains Road
Tarrytown, NY 10591-9001
Website: www.marshallcavendish.com

Library of Congress Cataloging-in-Publication Data
Stefoff, Rebecca, 1951–
Bears / Rebecca Stefoff.
p. cm. — (Animalways)
Includes bibliographical references (p.) and index.
ISBN 0-7614-1268-9
1. Bears—Juvenile literature. [1. Bears.] I. Title. II. Series.
QL737.C27 S69   2001   599.78—dc21   00-054668

Photo Research by Candlepants Incorporated

Cover Photo: *Peter Arnold, Inc.*: Thomas D. Mangelsen

The photographs in this book are used by permission and through the courtesy of *Photo
Researchers*: Alan & Sandy Carey, title page; Stephen J. Krasemann, 9; Tom McHugh, 13,
37 (top), 98; Jacana, 27, 73; Jeff Lepore, 37 (bottom), 57, 85; Dan Gurich, 41 (bottom);
Art Wolf, 44; Tim Davis, 51; Leonard Lee Rue III, 59; Tom & Pat Leeson, 63; George D.
Lepp, 67; B&C Alexander, 71; Jess R. Lee, 93; Alan D. Carey, 99; Tom & Pat Leeson, back
cover. *Peter Arnold, Inc.*: Ray Pfortner, 12; Thomas D. Mangelsen, 22; Fritz Polking, 33;
Heinz Plenge, 35, 68; S. J. Krasemann, 49; Roland Seitre, 52, 69; Klaus Jost, 65; Lynn
Rogers, 74, 79; Bios (Pu Tao), 96–97; *Corbis*: Archivo Iconographico, S.A., 15; Tom Bean,
16; Christie's Images, 19; Charles & Josette Lenars, 21; *North Carolina Museum of Artz*; 24.
Animals Animals: Zig Leszczynski, 40 (top), 81; Lynn Stone, 40 (bottom); Richard Sobo, 41
(top); Barabara Von Hoffman, 41 (bottom left); Stouffer Prod., 76; Leonard Lee Rue III,
83; Erwin & Peggy Bauer, 84, 88, 91.

Printed in Italy

1 3 5 6 4 2

Contents

Animal Kingdom

CNIDARIANS

coral

ARTHROPODS
(animals with jointed limbs and external skeleton)

MOLLUSKS

squid

CRUSTACEANS

crab

ARACHNIDS

spider

INSECTS

grasshopper

MYRIAPODS

centipede

CARNIVORES

BEAR

SEA MAMMALS

whale

PRIMATES

orangutan

HERBIVORES
(5 orders)

elephant

PHYLA

ANNELIDS

earthworm

CHORDATES
(animals with a dorsal nerve cord)

ECHINODERMS

starfish

SUB PHYLA

VERTEBRATES
(animals with a backbone)

CLASSES

FISH

fish

BIRDS

gull

MAMMALS

AMPHIBIANS

frog

REPTILES

snake

ORDERS

RODENTS

squirrel

INSECTIVORES

mole

MARSUPIALS

koala

SMALL MAMMALS
(several orders)

bat

1 "Greatest of Beasts"

An old story tells of a young woman who went out one day to gather berries. Darkness fell as the young woman walked back to her village, struggling with her heavy basket of berries. Suddenly, two young men appeared. They were dressed in bearskins. The men carried the young woman to their mountain home, where she discovered that they were really bears—spirit bears that could take on human form. They told her that she would have to marry one of them. Unable to escape, she agreed and married one of the bears. In time, she became the mother of twin boys who were half bear and half human.

Ever since she had disappeared, the woman's brothers had been looking for her. When they found her, they killed the bear who was her husband, but they let her two half-bear children live. According to some versions of this story, the dying bear told his wife's brothers the words to a magical song that would bring them good fortune as bear hunters. Other versions say that the

THE GRIZZLY BEAR, A TYPE OF NORTH AMERICAN BROWN BEAR, APPEARS IN THE LEGENDS OF MANY NATIVE AMERICAN PEOPLES.

woman's sons went back to her village with her. Able to take the forms of men or bears whenever they pleased, they grew up to become mighty hunters and great chieftains.

The native people of North America have many stories about the Bear Mother. The tale is also part of the folk heritage of traditional peoples in northern Eurasia. The entire northern world—from Scandinavia across Russia to Alaska and Canada—is home to the largest kinds of bears: black bears, brown bears, and polar bears. Throughout the northern world, wherever people have lived close to these powerful creatures, myths and legends about bears have been born. People have always felt a mysterious connection with bears, the fearsome yet fascinating creatures that share our world.

Bears and People

Scientists have identified eight different species, or types, of bears. One or more of these species is found on every continent except Africa, Australia and Antarctica. South America has only one bear species, which is only found in parts of the continent. In Europe, Asia, and North America, however, people and bears have existed in close contact for thousands of years.

Bears have always aroused the interest, awe, and respect of people. One reason is because bears are extremely challenging game animals. A hunter who killed a bear was sure of a big nutritious feast—but the hunt was risky. Bears are among the largest animals in northern Eurasia and North America, and they are very strong. Their long knifelike claws, sharp teeth, and powerful jaws make them fierce fighters. Although bears do not hunt people as food, these animals can respond with blinding speed and savage aggression if humans threaten or attack them.

Another reason that people are interested in bears is that

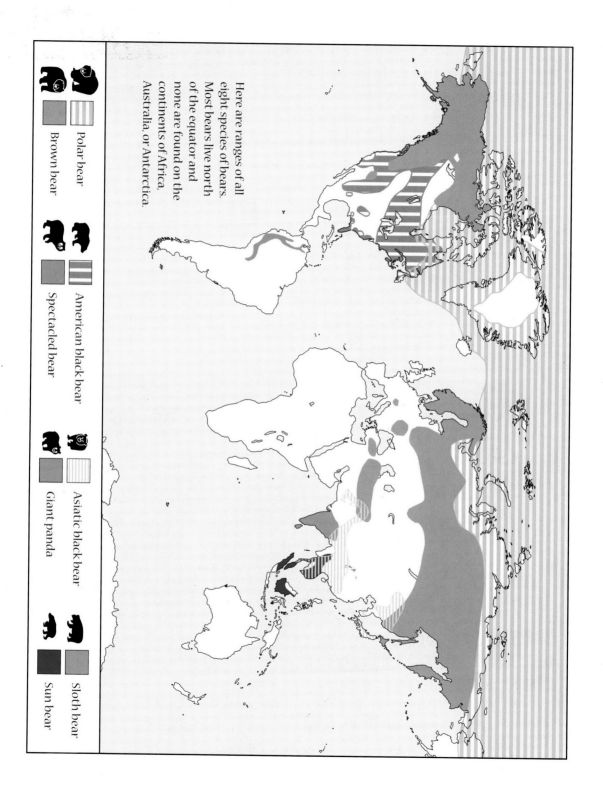

Here are ranges of all eight species of bears. Most bears live north of the equator and none are found on the continents of Africa, Australia, or Antarctica.

Polar bear

Brown bear

American black bear

Spectacled bear

Asiatic black bear

Giant panda

Sloth bear

Sun bear

bears sometimes seem similar to humans. Although bears generally walk on four legs, they often stand and occasionally walk on two legs, like people. Their footprints almost look like human footprints, but they are bigger and have claw marks in front. Bears, like people, eat both plants and meat. Unlike other animals, such as wolves, deer, and horses, bears often eat or handle objects with their forepaws, in much the same way that people use their hands. Bears also seem to show feelings, such as curiosity, anger, playfulness, and protectiveness toward their young—emotions that are familiar to humans. Most startling, perhaps, is the fact that the body of a dead bear that has been skinned looks like a human body. Some scholars who have studied the history of human ideas about bears think that this resemblance, more

A BEAR'S FOOTPRINT SPARKS THE IMAGINATION. IT CAN LOOK LIKE THAT OF A PERSON—OR OF SOMETHING ELSE. MANY SO-CALLED "BIGFOOT" PRINTS HAVE BEEN MADE BY BEARS.

ALL SPECIES OF BEARS OCCASIONALLY MOVE ABOUT ON TWO LEGS. THIS KODIAK
BEAR, A KIND OF BROWN BEAR FOUND ON SOME ALASKAN ISLANDS, SURVEYS THE
OCEAN.

than anything else, led to the early belief that people and bears were related—or that bears were a different kind of people.

The influence of bears upon people began long ago in *prehistoric* times. Between 100,000 and 35,000 years ago, two *mammals* that are now extinct lived in Europe. One was the European cave bear (Ursus spelaeus). *Paleontologists* believe that the cave bear, as massive as the biggest bears alive today, ate mostly vegetation. The remains of more than 100,000 of these bears have been found in European caves. The other mammal was *Homo neandertalensis*, or Neanderthal man, an early cousin of modern humans. The Neanderthals probably hunted cave bears, and they may have worshiped them or regarded them with special respect. Early in the twentieth century, Swiss and German scientists found cavebear skulls in two European caves. The skulls seemed to be carefully placed in hollows in the cave walls—although they might have moved into these positions through natural causes, such as flooding. The brown bear (Ursus arctos) also lived in Europe at the time, and bones of brown bears were found carefully placed in a pit that some experts think is a Neanderthal grave.

Modern humans, *Homo sapiens*, appeared in Eurasia about 35,000 years ago. These people began drawing and carving images of the animals in the world around them, including bears. Scientists think that most of the one hundred or so bears shown in Stone Age European art are brown bears, which were more numerous and had a wider range than cave bears. Unfortunately, no one knows for certain what these images mean. Many researchers think that the people who created the drawings believed they would bring good luck to hunters or honor the spirits of slain animals.

When people migrated, or moved, from Eurasia to the Americas about 15,000 years ago, they found bears there, too.

Over time, people in many parts of the world developed myths, stories, and beliefs about bears, passing them from generation to generation in rituals, stories, and, eventually, the written word.

The ancient Greeks had a myth about Salmoxis, a god of immortality (unending life), whose name meant "bearskin." Salmoxis was born in northern Greece and served as a slave. After gaining his freedom, he gathered followers, telling them that they did not have to die. He said that if they followed him they would live forever. One day, Salmoxis vanished into a deep cave. His followers thought that he was dead. Three years later, however, Salmoxis reappeared, proving that he had triumphed over death.

The myth of Salmoxis is probably based on an event that seemed to be a miracle to early people in Europe, northern Asia, and North America. During the winter, bears in these regions enter a sleeplike state called *dormancy*. They doze in caves or holes throughout the winter and wake up again in spring. To ancient people, it must have seemed as if these sleeping bears had died and then had been magically reborn. In many tales and customs, bears are symbols of immortality and rebirth.

When people moved from one stage of life—a form of rebirth—they held ceremonies that featured bears. The Indians of southern Minnesota, for example, called the initiation ritual that marked a boy's entry into manhood "making a bear." The boy had to dig a hole like a bear's den and stay in it for two days and two nights. After a mock battle in which men of the community pretended to kill the "bear," the youth could come forth, reborn as a man. In ancient Greece, girls on the verge of womanhood took part in a ritual called the *arkteia*, from *arktos*, the

THE FACE AND PAWS OF A BEAR APPEAR IN THIS TOTEM OF THE TLINGIT PEOPLE, WHO LIVE ALONG THE NORTHERN PACIFIC COAST OF NORTH AMERICA.

Greek word for "bear." In temples sacred to Artemis, the goddess of the hunt and protector of wild things, the young women—called "she-bears" during the initiation—feasted and danced. They wore brown robes so that they would look like bear cubs.

Bears came to be associated with certain supernatural beliefs and religious practices. Both the Gilyak people of Siberia and the Ainu people of northern Japan believed that bears were important representatives of the spirit world. The Gilyak thought that if a bear killed a human, the person's soul joined with the bear spirits that controlled hunting. Forever afterward, the dead Gilyak, now linked to the spirit realm, would look after the fortunes of his living relatives. The Ainu believed that all bears are related to a powerful being called the master of bears, who sometimes took the form of a very large bear and sometimes the form of a man. The master controlled the game animals that the Ainu hunted for food. The Ainu believed that when they slaughtered a bear, they were returning its soul to the master. They sometimes captured cubs, raised them for several years, and then killed them in sacrificial rituals.

Many Native Americans still believe that humans are guided and protected by animal spirits. Some groups believe that people are born with spirit guardians or inherit them from dead relatives. In other groups, individuals choose or identify their spirit guardians during initiation rituals. One of the most powerful Native American spirit guardians is the bear spirit—especially the spirit of the brown bear, often known as the grizzly bear in North America. In fact, some American Indians believe that the grizzly spirit is so powerful and unpredictable that it can be dangerous. Many Native American groups do not permit women to have grizzlies as their guardian spirits, and some groups avoid the bear spirits completely.

In 1908 Edward S. Curtis photographed a man of the Arikara people—
Native Americans of the northern Plains—wearing a bearskin. The
picture's title, *Bear Belly*, is a reminder that bears consume humans and, in
some myths, bring forth human descendants.

European Vikings of the seventh and eighth centuries also regarded bear spirits as fierce and dangerous. Bear spirits, the Vikings believed, could possess warriors during battle, making the fighters very strong and almost insanely brave. The Vikings called such warriors *berserkers*, from old northern words meaning "bear" and "shirt," because the men often wore bearskins into combat.

Other people also sought connections with the powerful spirits of bears. Among some hunting cultures in North America, Siberia, and northern Eurasia, people called shamans were thought to be able to communicate with the spirit world. The shamans were believed to be able to foretell the future, heal the sick, and provide spiritual guidance. Many shamans claimed to be guided or possessed by bear spirits. They often dressed in bearskins or wore the teeth and claws of bears. Bears were associated with healing, perhaps because they ate many of the plants used in traditional medicines. Shamans or healers sometimes touched sick people with bear claws or asked bear spirits to heal those who were suffering. To these people, bears were not just the mightiest animals known. They were also, because of their supposed powers over life and death, the most mysterious. As people crouched around a fire under the night sky, watching their bear-clad shaman dance in the flickering light, they could easily believe that the man possessed some of the bear's might and mystery.

Other beliefs about bears grew out of their resemblance to humans. Some stories, like the Bear Mother legend, told of bears who looked like men or women and married humans. The Inuit people of far northern North America, or Eskimos, believed that polar bears could become human by taking off their "bear suits" to enter houses. As soon as the "human" went outside and put on its bear suit again, it would become a bear

SOME CULTURES CREATE PERSONAL ORNAMENTS FROM BEAR PARTS. THIS DAYAK MAN FROM INDONESIA WEARS BEAR CLAWS IN HIS EARS.

POLAR BEARS, SAY SOME LEGENDS, COULD LIVE AMONG PEOPLE UNDETECTED BY TAKING OFF THEIR "BEAR SUITS."

once more. Some Native American legends claim that bears are the ancestors of the human race, or that the only difference between bears and people is that bears cannot make fire.

For both Native American and Eurasian hunters, killing a

bear was a serious matter. Some groups hunted bears only in special circumstances—when part of its body was required for a ceremony, for example. Others hunted bears regularly for meat, following special rules and rituals, such as asking the spirits to send dreams of a successful hunt. The hunters used terms of respect to refer to the bear. Siberian hunters called it Uncle of the Woods or Good Father. The people of Finland called it Golden Feet. Western Canada's Lillooet Indians sang over the bodies of bears they killed: "You were the first to die, greatest of beasts."

The people of many cultures in the Northern Hemisphere have imagined that they see bears in the night sky, in the constellations, or star patterns, near the Pole Star—the North Pole of the heavens. Two of those constellations are now called *Ursa Major* and *Ursa Minor*, Latin words meaning "big bear" and "little bear." In ancient Greek myth, Ursa Major was once Callisto, a woman loved by Zeus, king of the gods. Zeus's angry wife turned Callisto into a bear. The goddess Artemis killed Callisto, and Zeus sorrowfully placed the bear's body in the sky. Ursa Minor, the smaller bear constellation, is named for Arcas, the son of Callisto and Zeus. Halfway around the world, the Inuit people of Arctic North America also imagined that the stars of Ursa Major formed the shape of a bear—a bear that is being chased around and around the Pole Star by dogs that never catch it.

Fierce or Friendly?

Early beliefs emphasized the power and mystery of bears, even their dangerous, destructive force. When most people no longer had to fear bears in their daily lives, however, the image of bears changed. By the fourteenth century, for example, cities, towns, and farmland had spread across the European countryside, and bears were relatively rare. At about this time, images of stupid, lazy, greedy, or comical bears began to appear in folktales and poems. The awe that wild bears once inspired gave way to laughter at the antics of captive bears in circus-style entertainments. Stories such as "Goldilocks and the Three Bears," which was written in the nineteenth century, showed that even a little girl could outwit bears.

U.S. President Theodore "Teddy" Roosevelt launched a

BY THE LATE MIDDLE AGES, EUROPEANS HAD DRIVEN MOST BEARS OUT OF POPULATED LANDS. *THE BEAR HUNT*, PAINTED AROUND 1600, CAPTURES THE TERROR AND EXCITEMENT OF AN ENCOUNTER WITH ONE OF THESE INCREASINGLY RARE BEASTS.

new kind of bear image while on a hunting trip in Mississippi in 1902. When he arrived in the state, the president's hosts produced a black bear on a rope and invited him to shoot it—but Roosevelt would not shoot "that little fellow." Cartoons of the incident soon appeared across the land. Toy makers began selling small toy bears, calling them "teddy bears" to cash in on the presidential publicity. Teddy bears have since become one of the most beloved toys in history.

After the success of the teddy bear, bears became popular figures in children's entertainment. The most famous bear may be Winnie-the-Pooh, the hero of a 1926 book by British author A. A. Milne. The author's real-life inspiration was Winnie, a Canadian black bear who spent her life in the London Zoo. Other well-known bear characters include Smokey the Bear, created to teach children about fire prevention; Paddington Bear, hero of another children's book; Gentle Ben from the movie; and the cartoon bears Baloo, from *The Jungle Book*, and Yogi Bear. All of these imaginary bears are lovable, cuddly creatures. Real bears, however, are not. People who have encountered wild bears know that these animals possess the fearsome strength and unpredictable tempers that filled our ancestors with admiration and dread.

2 Yesterday and Today

Paleontologists have studied the fossils, or remains, of ancient bears found in many parts of the world. The bears we know today evolved, or changed gradually, over millions of years. During this long process of change, which is called *evolution*, new species of animals developed and others died out. Today, there are eight species of bears living in the world. The *ancestral* bears have long been extinct, but with the help of their remains, scientists can explain the similarities and differences among modern bears—and the relationships between bears and the rest of the animal kingdom.

THE FOSSIL SKULL OF *URSUS STOLEUS*, AN EXTINCT BEAR, GRINS MENACINGLY FROM THE PAST. AMONG THE EXTINCT BEAR SPECIES ARE THE LARGEST AND MOST PREDATORY BEARS THAT EVER LIVED, AS WELL AS MANY SMALLER VARIETIES.

Prehistoric Bears

Bears are members of the order, or category, of animals that scientists call the Carnivora, or meat-eating mammals. Most bears are primarily vegetarians, however. They belong to the order Carnivora because they share common ancestors with the other animals in that order. The ancestors of Carnivora lived about 65 million years ago, about the time that the dinosaurs became extinct.

These distant ancestors of today's bears were small tree-dwelling mammals called miacids. Some 60 million years ago or so, the miacid family divided into two branches. One branch evolved into groups of animals called the aeluroids or viverravines. Because this branch of the Carnivora includes all of the feline species, it is known as the cat branch. It also includes hyenas and mongooses.

The second branch of the Carnivora, which is called the dog branch, evolved into groups of animals called the arctoids or vulpavines. Paleontologists and zoologists (scientists who study animals) have grouped the many species that evolved from this branch into six families. Some of these species—including two entire families—have become extinct. Four families of arctoids still exist today. One arctoid family is the Canidae family of wolves and wild dogs. Another is the Procyonidae family of raccoons. The Mustelidae family includes weasels, stoats, skunks, badgers, and otters. The fourth family of arctoids is the Ursidae, or bears. Based on this evolutionary history, bears are closely related to dogs, raccoons, and weasels.

The evolutionary ties between bears and dogs are so close that one of the extinct families of arctoids is called the Amphicyonidae, or bear-dogs. The last of these animals, which combined the features of bears and dogs, disappeared about eight million years ago. By that time, the *ursids*, or members of the Ursidae family, were well established in many parts of the world. Scientists do not yet know much about the first ursids, although they think that their evolution began between 40 and 30 million years ago. The oldest known ursid fossils have been found in Asia and date from about 34 million years ago. They belong to a tree-dwelling animal the size of a dog that paleontologists have named *Cephalogale*. For many years, scientists thought that *Cephalogale* was an early member of the dog family, but it is now classified as a bear.

Few ursid fossils have been found dating from the period 34 million to 20 million years ago. Scientists do know that sea lions and walruses first appeared during this time and that these animals evolved from the ursids. Some paleontologists believe that the ancestor of today's sea lions and walruses was an early water bear similar to the polar bear.

Eurasian fossils from 22 to 20 million years ago show the emergence of a new species, *Ursavus elemensis*. This bear species is sometimes called "dawn bear" because all modern bears can be traced directly from it. Like the much older *Cephalogale*, the dawn bear was much smaller than any modern bear. It was about the size of a small dog, and scientists believe that it spent much of its life in trees. The teeth of *Cephalogale* and *Ursavus elemensis*, however, reveal an important difference between the two animals. *Cephalogale* was a true meat-eating *carnivore*. The dawn bear still possessed the cutting and tearing teeth that it needed to hunt and eat other animals, but it had also developed teeth for chewing and grinding, which means that it ate plants, too. Like modern bears, the dawn bear was an *omnivore*, an animal that eats both vegetation and meat.

The descendants of *Ursavus elemensis* gradually evolved into three groups. Zoologists call these groups subfamilies. The

Family Tree of Ursidae, or Bears

Polar bear

Brown bear

Asiatic
black bear

American
black bear

Sloth bear

European
cave bear

PRESENT

Small bear

URSINES

10 MILLION YEARS AGO

20 MILLION YEARS AGO

Sun bear

Spectacled
bear

Panda

Florida cave bear

Giant short-faced bear

T R E M A R C T I N E S

A I L U R O P O D S

Dawn bear

Doglike carnivore ancestor

subfamilies of the ursids are the ailuropods, the tremarctines, and the *ursines*. Many species in these subfamilies are now extinct. The eight species of bears alive today are their last remaining members.

The ailuropod group branched out from the family tree of the Ursidae about 20 million years ago, soon after the dawn bear appeared. Three million years ago, some ailuropods had evolved into pandas. The earliest panda types disappeared, but two species existed in Asia during the Pleistocene era, which began about two million years ago. One of them was *Ailuropoda microta*, which inhabited Southeast Asia but became extinct about 1 million years ago. The other species was the larger *Ailuropoda melanoleuca*, the giant panda, whose fossils have been found throughout China and as far south as Thailand. This species still survives today. The giant panda is the only living ailuropod.

Western scientists first examined the giant panda in the late nineteenth century, but they were puzzled as to how to classify it. In its Chinese homeland, the giant panda was called the bamboo bear because the Chinese people thought it was a kind of bear. Western scientists called it a panda because they thought it was closely related to the red panda, a much smaller animal that had already been classified as a member of the raccoon family. For a long time, the giant panda was regarded as a distant relative of the raccoon. In recent years, however, new techniques such as DNA testing have given zoologists a better

---

THE GIANT PANDA, LONG THOUGHT BY SCIENTISTS TO BE A LARGE MEMBER OF THE RACCOON FAMILY, IS THE LAST LIVING REPRESENTATIVE OF AN ANCIENT GROUP OF BEARS CALLED THE AILUROPODS.

understanding of pandas. Red pandas are procyonids, or raccoons, but giant pandas are the sole survivors of an ancient branch of the bear family.

The tremarctines were the second subfamily of bears to branch out from the ursid family tree. Paleontologists believe that they appeared in Eurasia about 15 to 12 million years ago. At that time, many forest regions were giving way to grasslands. The tremarctine bears *adapted* to this new environment. Because they had longer legs than earlier bears, they could run farther and faster when hunting the prey animals that grazed on the plains. By the beginning of the Pleistocene era, tremarctines had entered the Americas. Like other animals—and, later, humans—the tremarctines migrated from Siberia to Alaska during an ice age, when much of the world's water was locked into ice. At this time, the level of the oceans had dropped, exposing a land bridge between the continents where the Bering Sea is today.

Although the tremarctine bears died out in Eurasia, they flourished in the Americas. One widespread and successful species was *Arctodus simus*, the giant shortfaced bear. The massive creature measured eleven feet (3.3 m) when standing and weighed 1,300 pounds (600 kg). This bear was a meat eater and probably the fiercest hunter of its time. Scientists think that it was the largest carnivorous (meat-eating) mammal that has ever lived on land. Remains of the giant short-faced bear have been found across most of North America. In a few sites, scientists have found bones of the giant short-faced bear buried close to human remains. The earliest people in North America may have shared the continent with these huge bears—but not for long. The giant short-faced bear became extinct between about 20,000 and 10,000 years ago.

Another tremarctine bear, *Tremarctos floridanus*, may have lived even longer. Known as the Florida cave bear or the North

American spectacled bear, it ate mainly vegetation and lived in Mexico and the southern United States. A population of cave bears may have survived in Florida until as recently as only eight

THE SHY, RARE SPECTACLED BEAR OF SOUTH AMERICA IS THE ONLY SURVIVING MEMBER OF A GROUP CALLED THE TREMARCTINE BEARS. ITS EXTINCT RELATIVES— SOME OF THEM ENORMOUS—ONCE ROAMED NORTH AMERICA.

thousand years ago. A smaller relative of the Florida cave bear, *Tremarctos ornatus*, or the spectacled bear, adapted to life in forested mountain regions of South America, where it still lives. Like the giant panda, the spectacled bear—named for its distinctive markings—is the last representative of an ancient subfamily of bears.

The ursine bears, the third branch of the Ursidae family tree, evolved in Eurasia from *Ursavus elemensis* and its relatives. One of the animals that emerged during this stage of evolution was *Protursus*, which was larger than *Ursavus*—about the size of a modern wolf. About five or six million years ago, a bear called *Ursus minimus*, "small bear," appeared. The small bear is the oldest known member of the genus *Ursus*, the category to which six of the eight modern bear species belong.

Scientists are still sorting out the details of ursine evolution after the appearance of *Ursus minimus*. They think, however, that two groups of bears descended from *U. minimus*. One line of descent led to *Ursus etruscus*, the Etruscan bear, which evolved in Europe and spread throughout northern Eurasia. The Etruscan bear became extinct about 1.5 million years ago. One of its descendants was *Ursus spelaeus*, the cave bear, which evolved in Europe. Another was *Ursus arctos*, the brown bear, which probably evolved in China and then spread to Europe and North America. The cave bear became extinct about ten thousand years ago, but the brown bear still inhabits the Northern Hemisphere. The other line of descent from *Ursus minimus* led to black bears, including an early species that existed in North America about two million years ago. The modern survivors of this line are the Asiatic black bear (*Ursus thibetanus*), which lives in southern and eastern Asia, and the American black bear (*Ursus Americanus*), which lives in North America.

Two other ursine species live in southern Asia today. The

ASIATIC BLACK BEARS, INCLUDING THIS ANIMAL FROM THE HIMALAYAN REGION, ARE CLOSELY RELATED TO . . .

. . . AMERICAN BLACK BEARS, THE MOST COMMON BEARS IN NORTH AMERICA.

Malayan sun bear (*Ursus malayanus*) and the sloth bear (*Ursus ursinus*) are something of a mystery, however. Zoologists think that these bears descended directly from *Ursus minimus*, but they may have evolved from the Asiatic black bear or its immediate ancestors. Zoologists are more certain about the origins of the polar bear, *Ursus maritimus*, which is the youngest species of living bear. Polar bears evolved from brown bears in the Arctic. The earliest known polar bear fossils are only 100,000 years old.

Modern Bears

Since the first small bearlike creature crept along a tree branch 34 million years ago, many ancestral bear species have come and gone. The living legacy of the long process of ursid evolution is the eight species of modern bears that live in the world today. Because they share the same family history, the modern bears also share many characteristics. All have the same general body shape, for example. But the ailuropod bear, the tremarctine bear, and the six species of ursine bears each have distinctive features that set them apart from the others.

Giant panda. Since the middle of the twentieth century, when giant pandas began to be sent from China to foreign zoos, this once exotic black-and-white bear has become familiar to millions of people. With a round white face, black ears and eye patches, and a stocky white body with black shoulders and legs, the panda has the most dramatic coloring of any bear. The panda is one of the smaller types of bears. When standing on all four legs, it measures from 28 to 32 inches (70 to 80 cm) high at the shoulder and from five to six feet (1.5 to 1.8 m) long. Males weigh from 187 to 276 pounds (85 to 125 kg); females are slightly smaller, at 154 to 220 pounds (70 to 100 kg).

Pandas used to live in a large part of China and in Burma,

or Myanmar, on China's southern border. The increase in human activity in these areas, however, has drastically limited the panda's range. Wild pandas are forest dwellers, and vast tracts of the forests in which they once dwelt have been cut. Hunting has also reduced the number of pandas. Today, these ailuropod bears—the single species of this subfamily—survive only in a handful of isolated bamboo forests in remote mountainous districts of central and western China.

Spectacled bear. The spectacled bear is the only surviving species of tremarctine bear and the only bear native to South America. It has a shaggy coat that is dark brown or black with light tan markings around its eyes and across its nose. These markings sometimes look like a pair of eyeglasses, a fact that gave the spectacled bear its name. Often, however, the markings do not resemble spectacles at all. Instead, they may extend onto the bear's throat or chest. Male spectacled bears are 28 to 36 inches (70 to 90 cm) tall and from five to six feet (1.5 to 1.8 m) long. They may weigh from 220 to 342 pounds (100 to 155 kg). Female spectacled bears are about two-thirds as large as males.

The spectacled bear lives in the forested Andes mountains in the northwestern part of South America. It is found in Venezuela, Colombia, Ecuador, Bolivia, and, most frequently, in Peru. Scientists also believe that small populations of spectacled bears may live in Panama and northern Argentina.

Sun bear. The sun bear gets its name from the crescent-shaped patch of light yellow, tan, or gray fur that many individuals have on their chests. Some people think that this patch, which contrasts sharply with the bear's short glossy dark coat, looks like a rising sun. The sun bear is also called the honey bear because it frequently feeds on honey. It is also sometimes called the dog bear because it resembles a dog. The smallest living bear, the sun bear is 28 inches (70 cm) tall at the shoulder and

HERE ARE FIVE OF THE EIGHT SPECIES
OF MODERN BEARS. THEY HAVE
ADAPTED TO LIFE FROM THE TROPICS
TO ARCTIC ZONES. NOTE THEIR
DIFFERENCES AS WELL AS THE
CHARACTERISTICS THAT THEY SHARE.

Asiatic
sloth
bear

Brown bear

Moon bear

Sun bear

Polar bear

four to five feet (1.2 to 1.5 m) long. Sun bears may weigh 60 to 143 pounds (27 to 65 kg). Females are almost as large as males.

The sun bear is found in some of the most heavily forested areas of the Malay Peninsula, Sumatra, Borneo, Burma, Thailand, Laos, and Vietnam. Scientists believe that this bear's range was larger before an increase in human activity in the region—chiefly hunting and forest cutting—reduced it. For example, sun bears were once seen in the remote forests of China's southernmost province; but they have not been sighted there in recent years.

Sloth bear. The sloth bear is another small bear, 24 to 36 inches (60 to 90 cm) tall and five to six feet (1.5 to 1.9 m) long. Males weigh from 176 to 209 pounds (80 to 95 kg). Females are about two-thirds as heavy as males. The sloth bear's most recognizable feature is its long, shaggy coat, which is black, but can sometimes be shaded with tan or reddish tints. Its face is gray or light tan, as is the crescent-shaped patch on its chest. The sloth bear has long curved claws. This bear likes to hang from tree branches and generally moves slowly—features that it shares with tree-dwelling mammals called sloths. Until the early nineteenth century, in fact, the sloth bear was thought to be a type of sloth that looked like a bear, so it was called the "bear sloth." Its name was changed to "sloth bear" when scientists determined that it is really a bear that looks like a sloth. Like the sun bear, the sloth bear is also called the honey bear because it sometimes eats honey.

Sloth bears are native to all parts of India and the nearby island of Sri Lanka. They may also inhabit Bangladesh, Bhutan, and Nepal on India's northern border. In earlier centuries, the biggest threat to the sloth bear was hunting. Today, agriculture and other land-use developments are destroying the bear's habitat and reducing its range.

Asiatic black bear. The Asiatic black bear, sometimes called the moon bear or the Himalayan bear, is black except for its light muzzle and the white, gray, or light tan V-shaped marking across its chest. Another distinctive feature is the bear's extra-large ears. The Asiatic black bear is larger than the sun bear or the sloth bear. It is 4.25 to 6.25 feet (1.3 to 1.9 m) long. Males may weigh from 220 to 240 pounds (100 to 200 kg), about twice as much as females.

The range of the Asiatic black bear overlaps the ranges of the sun and sloth bears but it is larger than either of the other bears' ranges. Asiatic black bears live in mountainous regions of Afghanistan, Pakistan, India, Nepal, Bhutan, southern and northeastern China, Thailand, Laos, Cambodia, Vietnam, Mongolia, Korea, Japan, and Taiwan.

American black bear. The American black bear has a light-colored muzzle, like the Asiatic black bear, but it lacks the noticeable chest patch. American black bears may be from 4.25 to 6.25 feet (1.3 to 1.9 m) in length and from 32 to 28 inches (80 to 95 cm) in shoulder height. Adult males vary greatly in weight and overall size—they can weigh as little as 132 pounds (60 kg) or as much as 660 pounds (300 kg). Females are usually significantly smaller, sometimes only half as heavy as males.

The American black bear's range includes much of the North American continent, from Alaska and most of Canada in the north to northern Mexico in the south. The black bear once inhabited much of the United States, and its range still covers the Northwest, the Rocky Mountain zone, and part of California. In the East, the black bear is found from Maine to Florida, although its range has become limited and patchy in the eastern and central parts of the country.

As its name suggests, the American black bear is usually black, but not always. Its color can vary quite a lot, and bears

with brown or tan fur are common. Some strains of bears with variant coloring have been recognized as regional subspecies, or separate subgroups within the black bear species. These subspecies include the Kermode bear, a white-haired black bear found along the coast of British Columbia in Canada; the blue, silver, or glacier bear, a bluish black or dark gray version found in northern British Columbia and the Yukon; and the cinnamon bear, a reddish brown subspecies of southwestern Canada and the western United States.

Brown bear. The brown bear is the second-largest bear in the world, reaching lengths of 9.25 feet (2.8 m) and shoulder heights of 5 feet (1.5 m). Males weigh from 298 to 860 pounds (135 to 390 kg); females from 209 to 452 pounds (95 to 205 kg).

The brown bear's range is the largest of any bear species. At one time, brown bears lived throughout Europe, across northern and central Asia, and throughout western North America. Today, the largest unbroken stretches of the brown bear's range are in Turkey, northern and eastern Russia, central Asia, and northwestern Canada and Alaska. Some brown bears are still found, however, in parts of Scandinavia, southern and eastern Europe, northern Japan, and the Rocky Mountains of Canada and the United States. Not long ago, the brown bear's range was even larger. Until the nineteenth century, a population of brown bears lived in the mountains of Morocco in North Africa. The only bears in Africa, they probably descended from

CINNAMON BEARS ARE REDDISH BROWN IN COLOR BUT BELONG TO THE AMERICAN BLACK BEAR SPECIES. COLOR VARIATIONS OCCUR IN ALL BEAR SPECIES AND ARE MOST COMMON AMONG BROWN BEARS AND AMERICAN BLACK BEARS.

bears that crossed a land bridge from Europe during an ice age.

Like the American black bear, the brown bear has variable coloring. Shades range from light cream to tan, reddish brown, and very dark brown. Just as some black bears are brown, some brown bears are black. Color may not be a sure way to tell the two species apart, but the brown bear's shape is distinctive. A brown bear has a hump of muscle and fat between its shoulders. The line from its forehead to the end of its snout is somewhat concave, giving it a flattened, dish-shaped profile. Its long snout may appear to turn up slightly at the end.

The brown bear species has been divided into a number of smaller categories. Today, most zoologists recognize ten of these subspecies. Among them are the Eurasian brown bear; the Siberian bear; the red bear, found in northern India and the Himalayas; the Manchurian bear of northeastern China and Korea; the horse bear of Tibet and western China; the Hokkaido bear of northern Japan; and the Mexican bear. The Bajan bear lived in California and Mexico's Baja Peninsula until it became extinct in the 1920s. The Kodiak bear, the biggest of the brown-bear subspecies, lives on a handful of islands off the southwestern coast of Alaska. The tenth subspecies is the grizzly bear of Canada and the United States. The grizzly bear got its name because many individuals have coats with a grayish or "grizzled" appearance, caused by white or silver tips on brown hairs.

Polar bear. The largest of all living bears—and the largest land-dwelling carnivore in the world—is the polar bear. A typical adult male stands 5 feet (1.6 m) at the shoulder and may be up to eleven feet (3.3 m) long, weighing from 900 to 1,800 pounds (400 to 800 kg). Female polar bears are smaller but may weigh as much as 660 pounds (300 kg). The polar bear's most distinctive feature is its thick white or yellowish white fur. Under that fur, the polar bear's skin is black, as are its nose and paws.

Polar bears have long necks and heads that are smaller in proportion to their bodies than those of other bears.

Polar bears inhabit the Arctic region all around the North Pole. They live on land—on the Arctic islands, Greenland, and the northern fringes of North America, Norway, and Russia—and also on pack ice, the vast fields of ice that cover much of the Arctic Ocean and never melt completely. Far-roaming travelers and excellent swimmers, polar bears are often sighted on pack ice that is hundreds of miles or kilometers from the nearest land or swimming in the open sea. In winter, they may migrate south as far as Hudson Bay and Newfoundland in Canada, the Bering Sea coast of Alaska, and the Amur River of Siberia. Their summer range is farther north.

3 Bear Biology

All bears share a certain type of physical structure, or anatomy. They also have similar body functions, or physiology. Yet each species is set apart from the others by unique features and adaptations. Even the polar bear, the youngest of the bear species, gradually acquired a distinctive coloring and body shape that helps the animal survive in its native environment.

Anatomy of a Bear

The sturdy, stocky body of a bear is supported by a skeleton of thick, strong bone. The bear's skull shares many of the typical qualities of a carnivore's skull—for example, the jaws, which can open wide to grip prey, are surrounded by heavy, strong muscles that allow the animal to crunch bone, rip flesh, and pull or carry a heavy *carcass*. Bears, however, have evolved into omnivores, which means that they eat meat and vegetation. Their teeth differ

POLAR BEARS' FEET HAVE ADAPTED TO HELP THEM MOVE QUICKLY IN SPITE OF THEIR SIZE: TINY BUMPS ON THE PADS GIVE THEM GOOD TRACTION ON THE ICE, WHILE WEBBED TOES MAKE THEM EXCELLENT SWIMMERS.

in key ways from the teeth of true carnivores such as tigers. Bears still have the carnivore's sharp fanglike canine teeth, but their molars, or chewing teeth, are broader and flatter than those of true carnivores. The surfaces of these teeth are perfect for crushing and grinding plant matter.

Polar bears are the only modern bears whose diet consists mostly of meat. They have larger canines and smaller molars than other bear species. Sloth bears have forty teeth; the other seven species have forty-two. All bears lose their first set of "baby teeth," as humans and many other mammals do, but before the age of three, they acquire their permanent teeth.

Another important feature of the bear's skeletal structure is its foot, or paw. Bears have five toes on each paw—except the giant panda, which has six toes on each paw. The panda's sixth toe is not a true toe, however. It is a wrist bone that can move

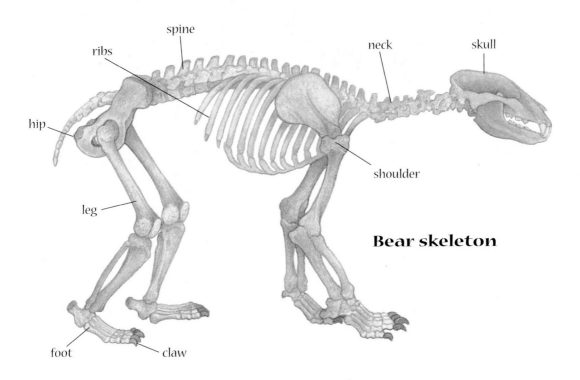

Bear skeleton

PANDAS, LIKE ALL BEARS, CAN CLIMB TREES. BEARS THAT ARE NOT TOO HEAVY TO REACH HIGH BRANCHES MAY SLEEP IN TREES OR SEARCH FOR FOOD IN THEM. YOUNG BEARS OFTEN TAKE TO THE TREES WHEN FRIGHTENED OR TO ESCAPE PREDATORS.

independently of the toes, almost like the thumb on a human hand. This feature helps pandas to handle the large bamboo stems that are their primary food.

All bears have claws on all four feet. Bear claws, like dog claws, are nonretractable, which means that they cannot be

A SUN BEAR CLAWS ITS WAY UP A TREE TRUNK IN MALAYSIA.

withdrawn into the feet like a cat's claws. Bears walk on all four feet but use only their front feet, or forefeet, for clawing, digging, or handling objects. Although a bear's hind feet are bigger than its forefeet, its fore claws tend to be longer than its hind claws. The sun bear, which spends much of its time climbing, has the sharpest and most curved claws of any of the bears. The sun bear's claws may be up to four inches (10 cm) long. A polar bear's claws are shorter but much thicker—sharp enough for hunting and strong enough for climbing on ice. Polar bears' feet have adapted to their Arctic environment, too. They are furrier than the feet of other species, for added warmth and traction on slippery ice. The toes are webbed along half their length, to make it easier for the bear to swim. The soles of the feet are covered with tiny bumps that improve the polar bear's grip on ice.

Bears' large feet, together with their short legs and heavy builds, give them a slow, lumbering walk. When bears want to move quickly, however, they can run at speeds of up to thirty-five miles (59 km) an hour.

Some prehistoric bears had long tails, like those of other carnivores. As the species evolved, however, ursid tails grew smaller until they almost disappeared. Sloth bears have the longest tails, about six to seven inches (15 to 17.5 cm). The average brown bear's tail is about four inches (10 cm) long. A story told by Native Americans in Alaska links the grizzly bear's stubby tail to its unpredictable, dangerous temper. According to the story, because the grizzly bear has lost his tail, he can no longer lash it back and forth when he becomes angry, as mountain lions do. The energy that once went into the bear's tail now goes into his legs instead, which causes him to charge at whatever upsets him.

The fur of a bear is one of the warmest, most insulating coats in the natural world, which is why bearskin cloaks and rugs are prized in many cultures. A bear's coat is made up of two types of hair. One is the soft, warm, fuzzy underfur. The other is the longer, shiny guard hair, which contains oil that repels water. A bear sheds both types of hair each spring or early summer, and new growth occurs. This process of shedding and regrowing fur is called molting. Bears look especially shaggy and unkempt during molting season. In bear country, tree bark is often festooned with tufts of fur that are rubbed off onto the trees by molting bears.

Digestion

An animal's digestive system allows the animal to take in food, break it down, and turn it into energy and waste. A bear's digestive system, like its teeth, reveals its carnivorous origins. The principal difference between the digestive systems of carnivores and *herbivores* (plant eaters) is that most herbivores have an extra stomach chamber—and sometimes more than one. In these chambers, the vegetation that the animal has chewed and swallowed undergoes a process called fermentation. This process breaks down the tough plant fibers so that they are easier for the animal's body to digest.

An herbivore's intestinal tract is also generally much longer than that of a carnivore. Food passes more slowly through the long tract of an herbivore, which allows the animal to absorb the most nutrients possible from the food it has eaten. Although bears are no longer true carnivores, they have not developed the extra fermentation chambers that herbivores have. A bear's intestinal tract is longer in proportion to its body than the tracts of most carnivores—but it is still shorter than the intestinal tract of an herbivore. As a result, a bear's digestion is not very efficient. This means that bears cannot live on tough grasses and

Bear organs

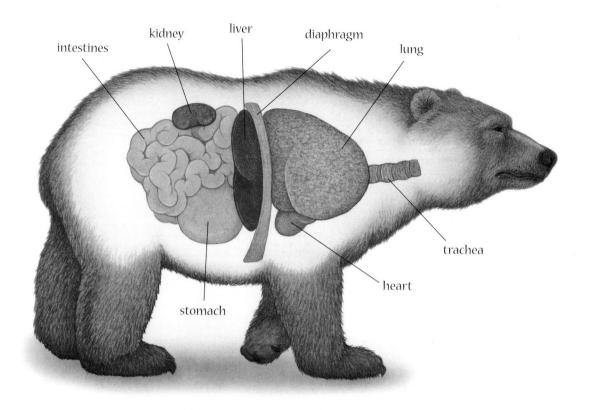

intestines · kidney · liver · diaphragm · lung · trachea · heart · stomach

twigs. Instead, they need to eat fruits and other plant foods that are rich in nutrients and easy to digest.

Reproduction

Bears have fewer young than many mammals. Female bears generally give birth to one to three cubs every two to four years. Because so few bears are born to each mother, the bear's reproductive system has adapted to increase each newborn cub's chances of survival.

Bears can reproduce successfully only if they are healthy

and well fed. When a male bear and female bear mate, the male's sperm fertilizes the female's egg. In most other mammals—a dog, cat, or human, for example—the fertilized egg then implants itself on the wall of the uterus and continues to develop as an embryo, in time becoming a young animal. In bears, however—along with weasels, sea lions, walruses, and red pandas—the fertilized egg does not automatically implant itself on the uterine wall. Instead, it may remain in the female's reproductive system for months before implanting. This process is called delayed implantation. Scientists are not sure what triggers the egg's eventual implantation, but they believe that delayed implantation allows bears to mate well in advance of the season when they give birth. It may also ensure that young bears will be born healthy. If the mother bear does not gain enough weight to nourish her young properly, the embryo never implants, and pregnancy does not occur.

The Senses

A bear perceives the world around it through its senses. Touch and taste are useful tools for examining objects close at hand, but the bear relies chiefly on sight, smell, and hearing. "Smell is the fundamental and most important sense a bear has," according to Stephen Herrero, author of *Bear Attacks*. "A bear's nose is its window into the world just as our eyes are."

Bears use smell to find food, to recognize and locate mates and cubs, to identify their own territory and the territories of other bears, and to avoid creatures that they prefer not to encounter, such as humans and other bears. Some zoologists think that bears may possess the keenest sense of smell in the animal kingdom. They have been known to catch the scent of prey many miles or kilometers away.

To a six-month-old grizzly cub, the world is full of scents. As young bears learn to use their powerful sense of smell to locate and identify food, they smell everything they encounter.

Bears were once thought to have poor vision, but many zoologists today believe that bears may have reasonably good eyesight, perhaps almost as good as human eyesight. Their night vision is probably even better than humans'. Bears can distinguish colors, and they have good depth perception, which means that they can judge how far away things are. They tend to be better at spotting moving objects than at noticing things that are standing still. Most bears are a little nearsighted, which means that they see objects that are close to them more clearly than they can see objects that are at a distance. The exception is the polar bear, which has sharp distance vision. The polar bear is also equipped with an extra eyelid to protect its eyes from the damaging glare of sunlight on ice and snow.

Although scientists have not yet proven it, they believe that bears have fairly good hearing, too. Wildlife biologists, hunters, and photographers claim that grizzly bears—the brown bears of North America—have the sharpest hearing of all the bear species. In his book, *The Grizzly Bear*, Thomas McNamee suggests that the grizzly's hearing is much sharper than that of humans. Grizzlies seem able to hear the movements of ground squirrels, pocket gophers, and other small animals in underbrush and underground tunnels.

Intelligence

Backwoods lore is filled with tales of bears' cunning. Hunters tell of bears that walk in streambeds to hide their tracks so that they cannot be followed. Bears have also been reported to backtrack, or retrace their steps by walking in their own tracks, to blur their trail. Polar bears have been known to cover their black noses with their white paws so that they would not be visible in a field of snow. Some researchers believe that bears sometimes use rocks or chunks of ice as weapons to strike seals or other prey. Brown bears, in particular, have a reputation for cleverness. Outdoorsman Enos Mills wrote in *The Grizzly—Our Greatest Wild Animal*, "I would give the grizzly first place in the animal world for brainpower."

THIS POLAR BEAR MAY SIMPLY BE COOLING OFF—OR IT MAY BE HIDING ITS BLACK NOSE AND PAWS IN THE SNOW, MAKING ITSELF "INVISIBLE" TO ANY TASTY HARES OR FOXES THAT ENTER THE AREA.

How intelligent are bears? Studies conducted at the University of Tennessee suggest that American black bears may be among the world's most intelligent mammals. They learn fairly quickly to solve simple problems, such as opening latched doors and unscrewing jar lids. Their nimble paws help them accomplish these tasks. Captive bears have even mastered many tricks—such as riding tricycles, a skill that doesn't always come easily to young humans.

Bears also have good memories and remember what they have learned. For example, years ago, bears living on the outskirts of a small Canadian town learned to associate the sight and sound of a big yellow garbage truck with the arrival of a new load of garbage at the town dump. On the day the truck made its rounds, bears would gather at the dump—even before the truck arrived to discharge its fragrant load. The bears' behavior continued until the townspeople started burying their garbage in a landfill far away.

Health Problems

Although well-fed bears are generally robust and healthy creatures, bears in the wild suffer from a variety of diseases, parasites, and health problems. Not all of these conditions are fatal, but they may contribute to overall poor health or prevent a bear from reproducing.

Anthrax (a bacterial infection that affects the lungs), blood poisoning, liver cancer, arthritis, pneumonia, rabies, and kidney infection are known to afflict wild bears. So is the disease tuberculosis, which is more common among polar bears than among any other species of bear. Digestive ailments are most common among pandas, which have the shortest digestive tracts of any bears yet eat the least-digestible food, bamboo.

About sixty types of parasites have been found on or in bears. Some of these parasites, such as ticks, fleas, and lice, are external. Most cause the animal nothing more than occasional discomfort. Bears can, however, be infected with bubonic plague by flea bites, just as people can. Nevertheless, internal parasites, such as tapeworms, hookworms, and liver flukes, are usually more serious than external ones. They can sap a bear's strength, making it more vulnerable to other illnesses. Perhaps the most widespread parasite is the trichina worm. Most polar bears and about three-quarters of brown bears are infested with this parasite. The infestation is called trichinosis, and it can kill the host animal if worm larvae travel into the animal's heart muscle or brain. Because the parasite lives in muscle, people who eat raw or lightly cooked bear meat, as is the custom in some Arctic cultures, are at risk for this potentially deadly disease.

4 How Bears Live

"Winnie-the-Pooh woke up suddenly in the middle of the night and listened," wrote A. A. Milne in *The House at Pooh Corner*. "Then he got out of bed, lit his candle, and stumped across the room to see if anybody was trying to get into his honey-cupboard, and they weren't, so he stumped back again, blew out his candle, and got into bed."

A snug, cozy den with a warm bed and an endless supply of sweet honey? Is this how bears really live? Some bears actually do sleep in dens and eat honey (although they don't, of course, have candles and cupboards). Other kinds of bears, however, have different living habits and styles. Bears have adapted to life in a wide range of environments, from tropical forests to Arctic ice.

No matter where they live, however, bears need a lot of fuel to keep their large bodies supplied with energy. Finding and consuming food is the main activity of a wild bear's day. Life in

LIVING THE GOOD LIFE, TO A PANDA, MEANS SITTING IN THE MIDDLE OF A BAMBOO GROVE AND CHEWING ALL DAY LONG.

the wild is also shaped by patterns of bear behavior that differ from species to species. An Alaskan brown bear and a Malayan sun bear, for example, spend their days, nights, and seasons in very different ways.

Finding Food

All bears are omnivores, which means that they eat food from both plant and animal sources. The proportion of plant food to animal food in a bear's diet varies from species to species. The bear's diet also depends upon what is available in a given place or season. According to some people, a bear's favorite food is whatever it can get. All species of bears have learned to take advantage of food sources introduced by humans: gardens, hen-houses, garbage dumps, trash cans, and coolers full of food in cars or tents at campsites.

Brown bears eat a mixed diet. About eighty percent of a North American grizzly bear's food comes from plants, including roots, leaves, acorns, berries, and fruit. Grizzlies have been known to consume at least two hundred different types of plants. The other twenty percent of their diet consists of animal foods, including honey (often with the bees), insects, worms, fish, rodents or other small mammals, and larger prey such as moose or deer. In addition to killing prey, brown bears eat carcasses they find or rob carcasses from other hunters, such as wolves. Diets vary depending on the brown bear's range. Brown bears in Tibet are more *predatory* and eat more meat than bears that live elsewhere. In Japan, brown bears are almost vegetarian. Eurasian brown bears tend to eat more ants than North American bears, which are more likely to dig for roots. In Alaska and Siberia's Kamchatka Peninsula, brown bears consume large quantities of fish. During the salmon's spawning season, when the fish crowd certain rivers, bears line the banks to snap up the swimming treats, sometimes catching sixty or more fish in a day.

BROWN BEARS CATCH SALMON AS THE FISH SWIM UP ALASKA'S BROOKS RIVER TO SPAWN.

Like brown bears, American black bears consume a varied diet. In spring, they fill up on tender young herbs and grasses. They also prey on wild animals as small as mice and as large as elk and moose (young or sickly animals are preferred because they are easier to catch and kill). Berries are a major food source in summer and fall, supplemented in the fall by fruits, such as apples, and by nuts, such as beechnuts, hazelnuts, chestnuts, and pine nuts. In all seasons, black bears are attracted to carcasses, to garbage, and sometimes to domestic livestock, especially young animals. The diet of the Asiatic black bear is similar to that of the American black bear—except that, as with brown bears, Asiatic black bears are more carnivorous in Tibet and more herbivorous in Japan. Asiatic and American black bears move around a lot during spring and summer, climbing up or down mountain slopes in search of the berries that are ripening at the time. Asiatic bears eat shoots, or new growths, of bamboo, which is not a typical food item in North America. They also eat more ants than American black bears do.

South America's spectacled bear is almost a vegetarian and will eat honey whenever it can. Spectacled bears may prey on animals when they can—this includes not only small game, such as mice and rabbits, but also livestock, such as calves, which makes these bears unpopular with farmers in their mountainous habitat. Like all bears, spectacled bears scavenge, or feed on, found carcasses. They also raid gardens for bananas, sugarcane, and other foods. Most spectacled bears, however, live on wild plant foods, including fruits, berries, and cacti. They have very strong jaws, which help them crack hard plant foods that most other animals cannot eat, such as palm nuts, tree bark, and the bulbs of orchids and other plants that grow on tropical trees. Spectacled bears climb into trees to feed. Once a tree's fruit has ripened, a bear may stay in that tree for several days. When the

Thorns cannot keep this American black bear from gorging on rose hips. Berries, seeds, buds, and other nutrient-rich plant foods are a vital part of the diet of brown and black bears.

SPECTACLED BEARS MAY SPEND DAYS AT A TIME HIGH IN THE BRANCHES OF TROPICAL TREES, EATING FRUIT, NUTS, AND EVEN BARK.

bear leaves the tree, it distributes the fruit seeds in its droppings. The survival of some tropical trees depends upon the spectacled bear's spreading of their seeds.

The sun bear of Southeast Asia may raid gardens or prey on livestock, but its diet consists mostly of earthworms, bees, and termites. One of the bear's favorite plant foods is the young buds of coconut palms. The sun bear has an extremely long tongue, which it sticks into termite nests or anthills to draw large numbers of insects into its mouth. The bear also inserts its tongue into beehives to lick honey. India's sloth bear also uses its long tongue to dine on termites and ants, its chief foods. The sloth bear catches insects in its own way, however: It knocks a hole in a termite mound, sticks its snout into the hole, and sucks like a vacuum cleaner, pulling in a mouthful of termites. The sloth bear also eats flowers, honey, grasses, and fruits.

The giant panda is the most specialized eater in the bear family. More than ninety-nine percent of a wild panda's diet consists of bamboo leaves and shoots. Because bamboo is not very nutritious and the panda's digestion is not very efficient, pandas must consume enormous amounts of bamboo to get the nutrients they need. Pandas in the wild spend about fourteen hours of each day eating, consuming from forty-five to eighty-five pounds (20 to 38 kg) of bamboo. These bears sit with their hind legs stretched in front of them and eat with their forefeet. In addition to the wrist bones that have evolved into thumbs, pandas have developed several other features suited to their

Sun bears are fond of coconut palm buds. They often eat ants and termites, as well.

diet. They have strong jaw muscles for chewing woody shoots and broad teeth for grinding them. Their stomachs are lined with a thick layer of mucus to protect the sensitive tissue from bamboo splinters. Pandas do not need an all-bamboo diet to survive, however—in zoos, they thrive on fruits, vegetables, and other plant foods, although they do best if their diet contains a lot of bamboo. Pandas are not hunters, but they sometimes catch and eat rodents.

Polar bears are the only bears that are almost entirely carnivorous. Their principal foods are ringed seals, bearded seals, fish, and crabs. They also occasionally, but rarely, prey on young walruses and whales. Polar bears digest fat more efficiently than they digest protein. For this reason, well-fed bears often eat just the blubber, or stored fat, from their prey. A hungry bear, however, will consume the meat, too. A polar bear does not always kill its own food—it will consume a carcass or eat garbage when it can. When polar bears do catch prey, however, they need to eat as much of it as they can, so they have very large stomachs. An adult bear can live off a single adult ringed seal for about eleven days. During the summer, some polar bears eat grass, berries, seaweed, and tiny water plants called algae.

Polar bears spend more time in the water than any other species of bear. Able to swim as far as sixty miles (96 km) without resting, they are the supreme swimmers of the bear world. All bears are good swimmers, though, and most species occasionally play in water or cool themselves in it—except for pandas, which avoid swimming whenever possible.

Night and Day Habits

Like most other animals, bears are active for part of each twenty-four-hour cycle and asleep for part of it. Schedules of sleep and wakefulness vary from species to species. They also vary with changing circumstances.

Sun bears, sloth bears, and spectacled bears are generally nocturnal, which means that they are active at night and asleep

Searching for seals, a polar bear peers into the icy waters of Spitsbergen, an island north of Norway.

during the day. Female sloth bears and their cubs, however, tend to feed during the day—perhaps because leopards and other predators that might harm the young bears prowl at night. Some scientists believe that spectacled bears that live in heavy forest areas may be diurnal, or active by day, but the details of these bears' lives are not well known.

Giant pandas may be active during day or night. Their schedule is dominated by the need to eat for many hours, whether it is dark or light. Asiatic black bears and polar bears, too, may be active by day or by night. Both species are thought to be more active at night and asleep through part of the day. Brown bears and American black bears tend to be most active at dawn and dusk, although when food is plentiful they will spend many daylight hours feeding. Both species tend to become nocturnal when they live close to towns or other sites of human activity. Bears in these areas have learned that if they move around at night rather than during the day, they are less likely to be seen and bothered by people.

All bears have day beds, where they can rest for a short time or sleep for a day or a night. Often a bear will have several such spots scattered throughout its feeding territory. The sun bear's day bed is a nest of broken branches in a tree, upon which the bear sprawls on its stomach. A spectacled bear also makes a nest. It rests sitting upright on a platform of branches, leaves, and twigs. Sloth bears make platform nests in trees, but during the rainy season—which can be severe in their native India— they seek drier shelter in caves. Pandas nest in caves or in hollows that they find under rocks or tree stumps; they also make beds of bamboo branches. Asiatic and American black bears sleep on tree limbs or on the ground in sheltered spots with soft vegetation. Brown bears use a similar type of day bed but they also dig shallow pits in the soil or in snow, sometimes lining them

A YOUNG EUROPEAN BROWN BEAR RELAXES IN ITS DAY BED.

with branches. Polar bears dig pits and burrows in ice, deep snow, or frozen ground. (Polar bears are the only bears that do not climb trees. All other species are good climbers, although brown bears become less agile in trees and less likely to climb as they grow older and heavier.)

Female pandas and sun, sloth, and spectacled bears often give birth to their young in their day beds, but they also give birth in dens. Dens are more secure shelters for the young cubs and may be either natural caves or holes dug by the bears. Female brown bears, polar bears, and both species of black bears give birth in dens. The den that a polar bear or brown bear digs usually consists of an entrance, a tunnel that is as wide as the bear's body, and a larger inner chamber. A brown bear can move as much as a ton of dirt while preparing a den. The Asiatic black bear looks for a cave or a good-sized hole in a hollow tree. Other bears may also use caves as dens, but often they dig their dens or enlarge natural holes that they find under logs or in trees.

Some bears use the same dens year after year. Others make or find a new den each year, perhaps even moving into another bear's old den. For bears that sleep through the winter, the den provides vital protection from harsh weather and enemies. A den is also a safe place for older bears to hide or escape from danger.

The Winter Sleep

During winter, food is scarce, so some bears spend those four to five months asleep in their dens. Many people describe these bears as hibernating, but that is not true in a scientific sense. The term hibernating describes how bats, woodchucks, marmots, and a number of rodents spend the winters. The body temperatures of hibernating animals fall far below normal, their heart rates slow, and their metabolic rates—the rate at which their bodies burn stored fat—also slow. Hibernating animals are hard to rouse and may not respond if disturbed. They wake up briefly from time to time to eat food they have tucked away in their burrows and to rid their bodies of wastes, returning quickly to hibernation. During winter sleep, bears do not experience great

HAVING GIVEN BIRTH DURING HER WINTER SLEEP, AN AMERICAN BROWN BEAR COMES OUT OF HER DEN, INTRODUCING HER THREE CUBS, ABOUT TWO AND A HALF MONTHS OLD, TO THE OUTSIDE WORLD.

changes in their body temperature, heart rate, or metabolism. They live entirely on their stored body fat and do not eat or pass wastes at all—although they do wake up briefly from time to time and move around. Scientists call the bear's winter sleep dormancy. Unlike true hibernators, dormant bears are relatively aware of their surroundings and waken quickly when they sense a threat.

Brown bears and most American black bears of both sexes are dormant in winter—in the warmer parts of the United States, however, male black bears remain active during winter.

A GRIZZLY HIBERNATES IN ITS DEN. THE BEAR IS IN A DEEP SLEEP, BUT IF DISTURBED IT MAY WAKE WITH STARTLING—AND DANGEROUS—SPEED.

Sun, sloth, and spectacled bears live in mild climates where food is available throughout the year. These species do not become dormant. The females, however, stay in their nests for several months while they are pregnant. During this time, they fast, or go without eating. Pandas do not become dormant and do not fast during pregnancy. Among polar bears, only pregnant females enter dormancy. Pregnant Asiatic black bears also become dormant, but other Asiatic black bears do so only in the colder parts of the range.

Bears prepare for their long winter sleep by eating as much as they can during the late summer and fall, trying to store enough fat to sustain their bodies through the winter. When spring comes, they emerge from their dens groggy, thirsty, and twenty-five to forty-five percent thinner than when they entered them. Yawning, scratching, stretching their stiff muscles, the newly awakened bears prepare for feeding and another cycle of seasons.

5 The Life Cycle

When a female bear comes out of her den in the spring-time, she may not be alone. If she was pregnant when she went into the den, she will bring her young cubs out into the world with her. The little bears have spent the first weeks or months of their lives in a familiar nest or den. They may blink when they enter the big, bright world outside. At first, they are timid, and their mother has to encourage them to venture forth on legs that may still be a little shaky—baby bears don't get much practice walking while in the den. Their awkwardness and fearfulness soon vanish, however. Bear cubs are active and curious, filled with energy and a desire to explore their sur-roundings. Still, they will stick close to their mother for at least half a year. She not only feeds and protects them but teaches them, too—and they have a lot to learn before beginning life on their own.

A THREE-MONTH-OLD AMERICAN BLACK BEAR CUB
TESTS ITS NEW TEETH ON AN ASPEN SAPLING.

Courtship and Mating

A bear's life begins with its parents' mating. Male and female bears do not mate for life or spend all of their time together. In fact, adult bears are solitary creatures. Each bear, male or female, lives alone in an area that scientists call its home range.

The size of a home range varies greatly from species to species, and even among different bears of the same species. In areas that do not have good food sources, for example, a bear must range over greater distances to feed itself. The range of a female bear is usually smaller than that of a male. Polar bears have the largest home ranges—from two thousand to as many as twenty thousand square miles (5,200 to 52,000 sq km). At the other extreme, the home ranges of pandas and the tropical bears are only a few square miles or kilometers because these bears can find enough food to eat in a fairly small area. An American black bear generally ranges over a few dozen square miles or kilometers; a grizzly bear's range covers a few hundred.

Bears do not defend these ranges as private territories—in fact, a bear's home range usually overlaps the ranges of other bears. Most bears maintain smaller core areas within their ranges, however, usually around their dens or favorite nesting spots. They defend these areas to keep other bears away from them.

Although bears sometimes gather in groups at food sources—for example, at salmon-spawning sites or around large carcasses—most of the time they avoid or ignore one another. When it is time for a female bear to mate, however, she gives off a scent that attracts a male. With most species of bears, mating takes place during a few days or weeks in spring or early summer. Sloth bears and sun bears, however, mate at any time of year. A female bear does not mate every year. The births of her cubs, called litters, are spaced two or three years apart. If the cubs die before the next breeding season, however, the female will mate the following year. Males can mate every year if they find a female.

Once a female's scent has attracted a male bear, he might have to approach her several times to see if she is ready to receive him. At first, her response may not be welcoming. She may snarl, strike him, or run away. If she is willing to take him as a mate, however, she will gradually accept his advances. Courtship behavior such as head bobbing, mock fighting, wrestling,

Grizzly bears nuzzling during courtship. Such behavior gives adult bears, who usually avoid one another, a chance to accept each other's company before they mate.

gentle nibbling, or hugging helps the two bears get used to each other. Some bears make courtship sounds, too—they may cluck, squeal, or bark. Pairs may remain together for a day or two, mating several times, or they may separate after a single union. Male bears of most species have no contact with females during pregnancy and take no part in raising their offspring—in fact, male brown bears, polar bears, and American black bears sometimes prey on young bears, including ones that they have fathered.

If the bears' mating is successful, the female becomes pregnant. The gestation period is the time that it takes for the young cub to grow from an embryo into a baby ready to be born. For all species of bears, this period lasts about two months. If northern bears were to give birth two months after mating, their young would be born in summer or fall—not the best time, as the bears need more time to build up their weight to survive the coming winter. Because of the female bear's delayed implantation, the fertilized egg does not begin to develop as an embryo until months after mating, when the bear is well fed. Northern bears that become dormant in winter give birth during their winter dormancy. The dormant bear rouses from her sleep to give birth and to lick and groom her newborn young. The bear species that do not become dormant usually give birth in their dens or day beds. They tend their young for several weeks or months before leaving the nest.

Bear Cubs

A bear's litter usually consists of one to three cubs. Occasionally, more cubs are born, but in these cases, some of the cubs are smaller and weaker than the others and usually die. All newborn bears are quite small compared to how large they will become as adults. Gary Brown, who served as a bear-management specialist with the National Park Service for many years, points out in *The Great Bear Almanac* that the weight of adult Kodiak brown bears is a thousand times that of newborn cubs. If newborn humans gained weight in the same proportion, the average grown-up would weigh 6,000 pounds (2,700 kg) or more! Bear cubs range from six to nine inches (17.5 to 22.5 cm) long. It's important that the cub gain a lot of weight in its early life. Fortunately, its mother's milk is very nutritious and contains much fat, which helps the baby grow quickly.

Newborn bears are bald or covered with fine fuzz. They grow their thick, plushy coats later. They cannot yet see, but they can sense warmth, which keeps them cuddled next to their mother. They can also smell milk, and their senses guide them to nurse from her body. For their first few weeks or months, the baby bears can only crawl, but they are ready to walk when the time comes for them to leave the den and begin their lives as young cubs.

At ten days old, this grizzly bear cub weighs thirty-one ounces (almost two pounds). Its eyes are still closed, and it spends its time nursing or sleeping.

Much of a bear cub's time is spent playing. Running, rough-housing, and other kinds of play help the young animals develop their eyesight, strength, and coordination. Play also gives them the chance to learn and practice skills that they will use later in life, such as swimming, digging, climbing trees, and stalking prey. Wrestling, head butting, and mock fighting are major play activities among siblings, or even among unrelated young bears whose mothers share the same range. Young bears continue play fighting until they reach about five years of age.

Cubs are deeply curious and are quick to investigate new sounds, sights, or smells. Their curiosity helps them learn—but

TEN-WEEK-OLD GRIZZLY CUBS CLING TO THEIR MOTHER'S BACK. THEY WILL SPEND AS LONG AS SEVERAL YEARS UNDER HER CARE BEFORE VENTURING INTO THE WORLD ON THEIR OWN.

A GRIZZLY CUB AT FIVE MONTHS OF AGE. BEAR CUBS' CURIOSITY AND ENERGY MAKE
THEM AMONG THE MOST PLAYFUL OF ALL YOUNG MAMMALS.

can also get them into trouble if they approach predators or fall into fast-moving river currents. Their mother, however, keeps a watchful eye on them. She also barks, clucks, or makes chuffing or woofing sounds to communicate with her young. The cubs recognize her voice over long distances and reply with calls of their own. Female bears are known for their strong protective instincts, and no bear fights more ferociously than a mother defending her young. Other adult bears, large predators such as mountain lions, and humans are the greatest threats to young cubs.

Aside from keeping her cubs safe, a mother bear's biggest job is teaching them how to find food. Cubs nurse from their mothers for varying periods: eight weeks for the fast-growing spectacled bears; about thirty weeks for American black bears; up to eighty-two weeks for brown bears; and 104 weeks for polar bears and Asiatic black bears. By the time they are weaned, or stop nursing, the cubs have already begun eating the typical foods of their species. At first, their mother brings the food to them; later, she guides the cubs to the food and shows them how to gather or catch it.

At the age of six to eight months, spectacled bears are ready for life apart from their mothers. Other species remain with their mothers considerably longer, from eighteen months to three years. The bear family finally breaks up when the female bear is ready to mate again. She leaves the cubs or drives them away. Often, bear siblings stay together for at least a year after they separate from their mothers.

Adult Bears

Once they are living on their own, bears establish their own home ranges and find or make day beds and dens. Female bears may mate for the first time and bear their first litters when they are three to seven years of age. Male bears may have to wait a few years longer to mate because older, more powerful bears may drive them away from the females.

Although they are solitary, bears are very aware of other bears in or near their ranges. All bears deliberately leave traces of their presence that other bears can see or smell. They do so by marking and scenting. Bears mark by scratching trees or rubbing against them and by depositing body wastes. Bears also have glands on their rumps that leave scents that other bears can recognize. These scent messages serve various purposes. They tell male bears when females are ready to mate, and they alert females that males are in the area. Through marking and scenting, bears also keep each other informed of their presence in overlapping ranges so that they can avoid one another.

When bears meet, one bear is dominant in the encounter and the other bear is subordinate. The subordinate bear recognizes the dominant bear as the more powerful or dangerous, and retreats. Older male bears are the most dominant, followed by females with young cubs. Males of any age are dominant over females without cubs. In an encounter between two males, the older bear is usually dominant. Sometimes, however, a younger bear may try to test its strength and claim the dominant role from a bear that is too old to win the fight.

During these encounters, bears communicate with sound and body language. They roar, hiss, and growl at one another and show aggression by standing upright. A direct stare is a sign of aggression and a threat. A subordinate bear generally lowers its head and looks away to show that it does not intend to fight. Most bear encounters involve only grunting and posing, and they end when one bear backs down and moves away. Sometimes, however, the encounter leads to a fight. Brown bears have been known to fight to the death. Battles usually

TWO KODIAK BEARS IN A SHOWDOWN FOR DOMINANCE.

involve males fighting over a female during the mating season or females fighting to protect their cubs from hungry males.

In the wild, most bears may live from eighteen to twenty-five years. Captive bears tend to live longer than wild ones because they are safe from predators and are well fed. The life spans of sloth bears and sun bears are not known for certain but are probably similar to those of other bears. Wild bears die of injuries and disease. They are killed in accidents, such as falling off cliffs or being crushed by boulders. If their teeth are worn or broken, or if they have gum diseases or painful mouth infections, older bears may be unable to eat and may starve to death. Few bears live long enough to die of old age, but a bear who enters dormancy or a winter season in poor condition may simply die in its sleep.

6 When Bears and People Meet

Humans have always shared the world with bears, but it is getting harder all the time for the two species to live together. When bears and people meet, sometimes people get hurt. Many people in the world today regard this risk as unacceptable. Bears are often regarded as dangerous pests and have been eliminated from many places where they once lived. Some scientists and wildlife managers want to reintroduce bears to the animals' former ranges—returning the grizzly bear to the national parks and forests of the American West, for example. Frightened or angry people who are living in these areas oppose these efforts, however. Today, humans are the primary threat to the survival of all species of bears.

A CAMPER WHO LEAVES FOOD IN A TENT MAY GET A SCARY SURPRISE UPON RETURNING. IN AREAS WITH A LOT OF HUMAN USE, BEARS QUICKLY LEARN THAT TENTS, COOLERS, AND CARS OFTEN CONTAIN FOOD.

Dangers to Humans

Nearly all bears, of all species, would rather avoid people than snack on them. Under certain circumstances, however, all bears are dangerous to people and may injure or kill them. Polar bears, the most aggressive and carnivorous bears, are most likely to regard humans as prey. Brown and black bears occasionally kill and eat the bodies of people that have threatened or attacked them, but they do not kill people just to eat them.

Most bear attacks occur when humans enter bear country and startle a bear or come upon it unexpectedly. The bear may respond by running away. On the other hand, it may stand tall and growl, just as it would when confronting another bear, or it may attack. A bear is most likely to show aggression or attack if it thinks that the person is trying to interfere with its cubs or with its food.

Bears of any species that have gotten used to the sight, sounds, and smells of humans are more dangerous than other bears. They are less likely to avoid people because people are no longer unfamiliar to them. If they have learned to associate people with food sources, such as garbage or picnic supplies, they are more likely to approach areas of human activity. The encounters that then often occur hurt both the people and the bears, which are often killed after they attack humans.

Anyone who is planning to travel, camp, or hike in bear country should get detailed information from officials of the park

A POLAR BEAR BEGGING FROM A TOUR BUS IN CHURCHILL, MANITOBA. SOME PARKS AND WILDLIFE TOURS USED TO FEED BEARS TO ENTERTAIN TOURISTS, BUT THIS PRACTICE IS DYING OUT. MOST EXPERTS AGREE THAT IT IS BETTER FOR BOTH BEARS AND HUMANS IF BEARS DO NOT ASSOCIATE PEOPLE WITH FOOD.

or forest services about how to prevent problem encounters with bears. One simple suggestion is to make noise, such as singing or talking, so that bears can hear you coming and avoid you. Local park or forest authorities can also provide guidelines that will help you keep bears from being drawn to your food or garbage. In some cases, it is enough to keep these items in your car; in others, you must hang the food or garbage from a tree branch or store it in a bear-proof container far from your campsite. Never leave food or garbage lying about and never sleep with food—or even the clothes you wore while cooking—in your tent.

Experts offer various advice on what to do if you come face to face with a bear. Many say that you should not run, because if you do, the bear may think of you as prey. The best thing to do is to murmur or talk quietly to the bear while you back away slowly. Do not look the bear in the eyes, however—the animal may regard this as a threatening stare. If the bear begins to follow you, try tossing a small object, such as a hat, off to one side. The bear may then be distracted enough to investigate the object while you continue your slow retreat. Some survivors of bear attacks claim that, if the bear does charge and attack you, the best strategy is to fall onto your stomach and play dead. Try not to move or cry out. Cover the back of your neck with your hands—an attacking bear will sometimes bite its victim's neck to break its spine. In most cases, a bear will lose interest in a creature that no longer appears to pose a threat, and it will simply wander off. Always seek the advice of wildlife or park authorities before entering bear territory. They will offer suggestions on what to do if you encounter a bear.

The best plan, however, is to avoid conflict in the first place by following safety precautions whenever you are in bear country. Above all, never approach a bear, even if you are in the middle of a national park and the animal looks tame! Tourists in Yellowstone National Park have been injured while trying to feed bears by hand or take pictures of their cubs. No photo opportunity is worth taking such foolish risks.

Threats to Bears

Stories of bears attacking humans are horrifying, but people do far more damage to bears than bears do to people. People kill bears directly by hunting and indirectly by changing or destroying their natural habitat. Most bear populations are shrinking, and bears have lost between half and three-quarters of their native range worldwide. Some bear species are now at risk of becoming extinct.

The Convention on International Trade in Endangered Species (CITES) lists species that are currently endangered and those that could become endangered if the present trends continue. According to CITES, five of the eight species of bear are endangered. One of these is the giant panda, the rarest of bears. There are about 1,100 of these animals living in the wild, and about one hundred living in zoos. The World Wildlife Fund (WWF), an organization that works to protect wild animals and their habitats, has adopted the panda as its symbol of conservation. The plight of the panda represents the plight of all endangered species.

The other endangered bear species are the spectacled bear, with an estimated one to two thousand in the wild and another 150 or so living in zoos; the sun bear, whose numbers are not known but whose population has decreased greatly in recent years; the sloth bear, which is vanishing fast, with only some seven to ten thousand bears remaining in the wild; and the Asiatic black bear, whose population is also shrinking rapidly.

THE PANDA, THE
RAREST BEAR, HAS
BECOME A SYMBOL OF
ENDANGERED SPECIES
EVERYWHERE.

All bears suffer when their habitat is reduced through human activities such as logging. Tropical bears living in areas of rapid population growth, such as this sun bear from Southeast Asia, are in greatest danger.

Some fifty thousand brown bears remain in North America, most of them in western Canada and Alaska. There may be as many as 100,000 of them in Eurasia, but 70,000 are in Russia and Central Asia, where little effort is made to protect and preserve them. Bear populations in Scandinavia and western Europe are broken up and isolated on small "islands" of remaining habitat in mountain regions. Many of these populations are at serious risk of disappearing. Some—but not all—countries with brown-bear populations have laws that protect them. Estimates of the

THE SLOTH BEAR OF INDIA IS AN ENDANGERED SPECIES—WITH ONLY SEVEN TO TEN THOUSAND REMAINING IN THE WILD.

numbers of polar bears in the wild range from 5,000 to 20,000. Polar bears are not officially endangered, but CITES has listed them as vulnerable. The countries in which these bears live have passed laws to ban or control hunting. The species with the healthiest population is the American black bear, which may number as many as 400,000 or 500,000 individuals in the wild. Although some regional subspecies have declined and others have become extinct, the population has actually increased in some parts of the black bear's range.

Hunting is a serious threat to several bear species, especially Asiatic black bears and sun bears. Why do people hunt and kill bears? Sometimes they do so because they regard bears as pests that threaten their crops or livestock. Occasionally, people kill bears for meat. Others hunt bears for sport—a wild bear is one of the most impressive game trophies that a hunter can display. Sometimes, bears are slaughtered because of the mistaken belief that parts of their bodies have medicinal or magical powers.

People have long thought that by consuming some part of a bear's body they could gain the bear's strength and vigor. Hunters of the Native American Kwakiutl people of the Pacific Northwest, for example, thought that by killing and consuming a grizzly bear they would acquire the fierceness and fishing skill of the grizzly. Such beliefs had magical or religious origins and did no lasting harm when bear populations were large. Bear parts, especially gallbladders and penises, were also used in various forms of traditional Asian medicine. Although these remedies have no proven medical benefit, they remain popular in Asia— unfortunately for the bears, who are killed in large numbers to supply the demand for "medicinal" body parts. Because of the bears' endangered status, the trade in such parts is illegal in many countries, but it continues anyway, and it has spread beyond Asian bear species. Wildlife officials in the western

United States have arrested hunters for slaughtering black bears without proper hunting permits. These hunters then strip the carcasses of gallbladders and penises, which are undoubtedly destined for the Asian-medicine trade.

AMERICAN BLACK BEARS, SUCH AS THIS AMERICAN CINNAMON BEAR, ARE STILL NUMEROUS, AND SCIENTISTS SAY THAT THEY ARE IN NO IMMEDIATE DANGER OF EXTINCTION. STILL, HUNTING—OFTEN TO SATISFY A SUPERSTITIOUS MARKET FOR BEAR PARTS—HAS BECOME A THREAT TO THESE BEARS AS WELL AS TO THEIR ASIAN COUSINS. WITHOUT PROTECTION, WILD BEARS MAY SOMEDAY BE CREATURES ONLY OF HISTORY, LEGEND, AND MYTH.

Bears need room to live, and the increase in human activities such as farming, forestry, and mining is taking that room away. Tree-dwelling tropical bears lose habitat when forests are cut down—a particularly serious threat in Southeast Asia, where the human population is growing rapidly. When their natural homes are destroyed, bears generally find themselves living closer to humans than they did before. These bears are then likely to be killed as dangerous pests by the people who destroyed their habitat in the first place.

Wildlife biologists and conservation experts agree that the key to the survival of bears in our world is international cooperation. All countries must agree to protect endangered bears, set aside places for them to live and breed, and crack down on illegal hunting and the trade in illegal bear products. If not, bears may one day exist only in zoos, and the wild bear—the magnificent creature that inspired prehistoric cave painters and was once thought to live forever—will be a thing of the past.

Glossary

The following words appear in this book. Some are "bear words," and others are more general terms from the sciences, especially biology.

adapt—change or develop in ways that aid survival in the environment

ancestral—having to do with lines of descent or earlier forms

carcass—body of a dead animal

carnivore—animal that eats meat

dormancy—period of extended sleep or greatly reduced activity

Eurasia—landmass formed by the continents of Europe and Asia. (Geographers consider Russia's Ural Mountains to be the boundary between the continents.)

evolution—process by which species, or types of plants and animals, change over time, with new species emerging and old ones dying out

extinct—no longer in existence; died out

habitat—type of environment in which an animal lives

herbivore—animal that eats plants

mammal—animal with a backbone that nourishes its young with milk from its mammary glands. Bears and humans are mammals, as are thousands of other animals.

omnivore—animal that eats both plants and meat

paleontologist—scientist who practices palentology, the study of ancient and extinct life forms, usually by examining fossil remains

predatory—having to do with predation, the act of killing for food

prehistoric—the time period before the invention of writing and the beginning of written history

ursid—member of the family of Ursidae, which includes all living and extinct bears

ursine—having to do with bears

Species Checklist

The list below identifies the eight bear species living in the world today. They include one ailuropod, one tremarctine, and six ursine species. The scientific name, common name, and range have been provided for each one.

Scientific name	Common name	Range
Ailuropoda melanoleuca	Giant panda	China
Tremarctos ornatus	Spectacled bear	South America
Ursus malayanus (also *Helarctos malayanus*)	Sun bear	Southeast Asia
Ursus ursinus (also *Melursus ursinus*)	Sloth bear	South Asia
Ursus thibetanus (also *Arctos* or *Selenarctos thibetanus*)	Asiatic black bear (sometimes called moon bear)	South, Southeast, and East Asia
Ursus americanus	American black bear	North America
Ursus arctos	Brown bear (sometimes called Kodiak bear or grizzly bear)	Northern Eurasia and Northwestern North America
Ursus maritimus	Polar bear	Arctic Region

Further Research

The books listed here are just a small fraction of the many volumes about bears available in libraries and bookstores. A selection of videos and Web sites about bears is also included.

Books for Young People

Barrett, Norman S. *Bears*. New York: Franklin Watts, 1988.

DuTemple, Lesley A. *Polar Bears*. Minneapolis: Lerner, 1997.

Greenaway, Theresa. *Amazing Bears*. New York: Knopf, 1992.

Harrison, Virginia. *The World of Polar Bears*. Milwaukee: Gareth Stevens, 1989.

Kulling, Monica. *Bears: Life in the Wild*. New York: Golden Books, 1998.

Macdonald, Mary Ann. *Grizzlies*. Plymouth, MN: Child's World, 1997.

Markle, Sandra. *Growing Up Wild: Bears*. New York: Atheneum Books for Young Readers, 2000.

Miller, Debbie S. *A Polar Bear Journey*. Boston: Little, Brown, 1997.

Moore, Tara. *Polar Bears*. Champaign, IL: Garrard, 1982.

Nentl, Jerolyn A. *The Grizzly*. Mankato, MN: Baker Street Productions, 1984.

Patent, Dorothy Hinshaw. *Bears of the World*. New York: Holiday House, 1980.

———. *The Great Ice Bear*. New York: Morrow Junior Books, 1999.

———. *The Way of the Grizzly*. New York: Clarion, 1987.

Pfeffer, Wendy. *Polar Bears*. Parsippany, NJ: Silver Press, 1997.

Pluckrose, Henry, editor. *Bears*. New York: Gloucester Press, 1979.

Pringle, Laurence P. *Bearman: Exploring the World of Black Bears*. New York: Scribner's, 1989.

Rosenthal, Mark. *Bears*. Chicago: Children's Press, 1983.

Silverstein, Alvin. *The Grizzly Bear*. Brookfield, CT: Millbrook Press, 1998.

Stirling, Ian. *Bears*. San Francisco: Sierra Club Books for Children, 1992.

Stone, Lynn M. *Grizzlies*. Minneapolis:Carolrhoda Books, 1993.

Whittaker, Bibby. *A Closer Look at Bears and Pandas*. New York: Gloucester Press, 1986.

Videos

All American Bear. Nova Video Library, 1988.

Bear. BBC Worldwide Americas, 1997.

Ghost Bears. PBS-WNET, 1995.

Giant Bears of Kodiak Island. National Geographic Video, 1994.

The Great Bears of Alaska. Discovery Communications, 1993.

Grizzly and Man: Uneasy Truce. National Audobon Video, 1988.

Polar Bear Alert. National Geographic Society Educational Services, 1987.

Secrets of the Wild Panda. National Geographic Video, 1994.

Web Sites

www.americanbear.org is the official home page of the American Bear Association, a nonprofit organization whose mission is "to promote the well-being of black bears, other wildlife, and all natural resources through a better understanding." Contains bear facts, photographs, and links to other sites.

www.bear.org is the home page of the North American Bear Center, a clearinghouse for bear information and conservation news, with a children's page and links to other sites.

www.brownbear.org contains photographs and information about the grizzly bear. This site also contains information about habitats and efforts to protect this endangered species.

www.nature-net.com/bears/index.html is the home page of The Bear Den, an award-winning site that its owner says is "for bears everywhere, and for those humans who are on their side." The site contains information about the eight bear species, bear-related news items, a children's section, photographs, and links to other sites.

www.polarbearsalive.org is the home page of a nonprofit organization dedicated to protecting polar bears and their natural habitats.

Bibliography

These books were especially useful to the author in researching this book. They are good sources of interesting and entertaining information about bears for the general reader.

Brown, Gary. *The Great Bear Almanac*. New York: Lyons and Burford, 1993. Detailed but readable survey of all bear species by a former bear-management specialist with the National Park Service. Good overview of bear biology. Many lists and tables of facts. Color photographs and black-and-white drawings.

Cox, Daniel J. *Black Bear*. San Francisco: Chronicle Books, 1990. Collection of color photographs that illustrate the life and habits of the most common American bear.

East, Ben. *Bears*. New York: Crown, 1977. Stories of bear encounters told by longtime hunter and outdoorsman.

Feazel, Charles T. *White Bear: Encounter with the Master of the Arctic Ice*. New York: Henry Holt, 1990. Review of history, myths, and scientific research about polar bears. Emphasis on threats to bears' survival. Black-and-white photographs.

Schaller, George B. *The Last Panda*. Chicago: University of Chicago Press, 1993. World-famous wildlife biologist reports on research on pandas in their natural habitat and asks, Will wild pandas survive? Color photographs. Schullery, Paul, edit. Mark of the Bear: Legend and Lore of an American Icon. San Francsico: Sierra Club Books, 1996. Essays about black, brown, and polar bears by ten American nature writers. Color photographs.

Shepard, Paul and Barry Sanders. *The Sacred Paw: The Bear in Nature, Myth, and Literature*. New York: Viking, 1985. Review of the various meanings that bears have held for people. Chapter on bears in literature is especially interesting. Black-and-white photographs.

Stirling, Ian. *Polar Bears*. Ann Arbor: University of Michigan Press, 1988. Blends scientific knowledge with the bear lore of the North American Arctic people known as the Inuit, whose culture and environment are well described. Outstanding color photographs.

Ward, Paul and Suzanne Kynaston. *Bears of the World*. London: Blandford, 1999. Handy reference guide to bear species, evolution, and behavior. Includes a very good chapter on bears in religion, mythology, and folklore. Color photographs.

Index

Page numbers for illustrations are in **boldface**.

About the Author

Rebecca Stefoff has written many books on scientific and historical subjects for children and young adults. Among them are *Horses* in Marshall Cavendish's Animal Ways series and the eighteen volumes of the Living Things series, also published by Marshall Cavendish. Stefoff lives in Portland, Oregon, and has had several encounters—peaceful but exciting—with black bears during camping and hiking trips in the West.